30 Days to Holistic Healing

A Path to Wholeness and Well-being

Krista Buda, LCSW

This book is dedicated to the survivors who are working hard to take back their life and find their healing. To the healers out there who love and care. Most of all to my loving partner Trisan, who supports all the energy I pour into being a healer and supports my healing in so many ways.

Acknowledgements

The creation of this workbook has been greatly enriched by the invaluable insights and wisdom generously shared by numerous healers and trainers. Heartfelt gratitude is extended to the esteemed institutions, including Boston University, Quantum University, the International Psychiatry Institute, EMDRIA, and the vibrant communities who have generously imparted their profound knowledge. Among these contributors are several Cuanderas from Peru, Ayurvedic Practitioners, Traditional Chinese Medicine healers, Yogis, and many others whose collective wisdom has played an instrumental role in shaping the content of this work.

Table of Contents

Introduction to Holistic Healing for PTSD

Post-Traumatic Stress Disorder (PTSD) is a complex and challenging condition that can deeply affect the lives of those who experience it. It often arises in response to traumatic events, leaving individuals with emotional, psychological, and physical scars that can be difficult to heal. While traditional approaches to PTSD treatment, such as therapy and medication, have shown effectiveness, a growing number of individuals are exploring holistic healing as a complementary or alternative option.

Holistic healing for PTSD acknowledges the interconnectedness of the mind, body, and spirit. It embraces a comprehensive approach to well-being that seeks to address not only the symptoms of PTSD but also the underlying imbalances that contribute to its persistence. This holistic perspective recognizes that trauma impacts every aspect of a person's life, and as such, healing should encompass various dimensions: emotional, physical, social, and spiritual.

In this guide, we will explore holistic healing modalities and strategies that can complement traditional PTSD treatments. From mindfulness practices to nutrition, movement, and alternative therapies, we will delve into a holistic approach that empowers individuals to engage in their own healing journey. It's important to note that holistic healing is not a replacement for conventional treatments but can serve as a valuable adjunct, helping individuals find balance, resilience, and a sense of wholeness as they work towards recovery from PTSD.

Day 1: Understanding PTSD

Deciphering PTSD: Facts, Statistics, Causes, and Consequences

Post-Traumatic Stress Disorder (PTSD) is a multifaceted mental health condition with profound effects on individuals. In this chapter, we will delve into the fundamental aspects of PTSD, shedding light on its prevalence, underlying triggers, and potential repercussions.

Unraveling PTSD

Defining PTSD

Post-Traumatic Stress Disorder is a psychiatric condition that can develop after an individual has endured or witnessed a traumatic event. Such events can encompass a wide range, including combat experiences, natural disasters, accidents, sexual or physical assault, or any situation that poses a significant threat to one's life. PTSD is characterized by enduring symptoms that persist well beyond the traumatic incident.

Prevalence and Figures

PTSD is a relatively common mental health issue, affecting a substantial number of individuals worldwide.

According to the National Institute of Mental Health (NIMH), approximately 3.6% of U.S. adults aged 18-54 experience PTSD in any given year.

It is estimated that around 7-8% of the population will grapple with PTSD at some point during their lives.

Veterans and survivors of military conflicts face a heightened risk, with an estimated 11-20% being affected by PTSD.

Notably, women are more susceptible to PTSD than men.

Roots of PTSD

Traumatic Triggers

The primary catalyst for PTSD is exposure to traumatic events. These events can take myriad forms and may involve:

- Combat situations and the traumas associated with warfare.
- Instances of physical or sexual assault.
- Natural disasters, including earthquakes, hurricanes, or wildfires.
- Severe accidents, such as vehicular crashes or industrial mishaps.
- Traumatic experiences during childhood, like abuse or neglect.
- Bearing witness to traumatic incidents happening to others.

Risk Factors

Not everyone exposed to trauma develops PTSD; several risk factors play a role, including:

- The gravity and duration of the traumatic event.
- Individual susceptibility, encompassing genetic factors and family history.

- The presence of social support systems.

- Pre-existing mental health conditions.

- Substance abuse or dependence.

Ramifications and Effects of PTSD

Symptoms of PTSD

PTSD exhibits itself through a diverse array of symptoms, including:

- Intrusive thoughts, recurrent flashbacks, or distressing nightmares related to the traumatic event.

- Vigilant avoidance of reminders of the trauma, such as locations, individuals, or activities.

- Adverse changes in mood or cognition, such as persistently negative beliefs or distorted feelings of guilt.

- Heightened arousal, characterized by irritability, sleep disturbances, and heightened startle responses.

Impact on Daily Life

PTSD can substantially impede an individual's daily functioning and overall well-being. It may disrupt relationships, work, and personal contentment. Those with PTSD may encounter challenges such as substance abuse, feelings of isolation, and difficulties maintaining employment.

Long-Term Consequences

In the absence of adequate treatment, PTSD can lead to enduring repercussions, including:

- Persistent physical health issues like cardiovascular diseases or autoimmune disorders.
- Elevated vulnerability to other mental health disorders, such as depression and anxiety.
- An increased propensity for engaging in risky behaviors, including self-harm or substance abuse.
- Social withdrawal and strained interpersonal relationships.
- An overall diminished quality of life.

Gaining a comprehensive grasp of the facts, statistics, causes, and consequences of PTSD lays the foundation for addressing this intricate condition. Subsequent chapters will delve into holistic approaches, conventional treatments, and coping strategies, offering guidance to individuals embarking on their path to healing and recovery.

30-DAY SELF-HELP

ACTIVITIES

Welcome to "30 Days to Holistic Healing: A Path to Wholeness and Well-Being." This self-help book is your gateway to a transformative journey, a voyage of self-discovery, and a blueprint for implementing holistic strategies that will nurture your body, mind, and spirit. As you embark on this 30-day adventure, you are taking a profound step towards reclaiming your well-being, finding balance, and unlocking the potential for deep healing. Throughout the next 30 days, you will explore a diverse range of holistic strategies, each designed to empower you to take charge of your well-being. From mindfulness and nutrition to movement and self-expression, we will delve into various aspects of holistic healing. You will learn how to nurture your body with wholesome foods, calm your mind through meditation, embrace the healing power of nature, and strengthen your emotional resilience.

But remember, healing is a deeply personal and individual journey. You are encouraged to approach these 30 days with an open heart and an open mind. Your unique experiences, challenges, and triumphs will shape this journey, making it your own. If you ever feel overwhelmed or miss a day, that's perfectly okay—compassion for yourself is a vital part of holistic healing.

So, as you turn the page and begin your first day of holistic healing, know that you are embarking on a path that has the potential to lead you to a place of profound well-being, balance, and vitality. Your commitment to this journey is a testament to your inner strength and your desire for a healthier, happier, and more harmonious life. Let's take this step forward together, embracing the holistic strategies that can lead us to a life of holistic healing.

Day 1: Understanding PTSD Assignment:

Journal your experiences with PTSD. What traumatic events have you experienced? How do they affect you today?

Day 2: The Mind-Body Connection

Healing from Post-Traumatic Stress Disorder (PTSD) involves recognizing and harnessing the profound connection between the mind and the body. Our mental and emotional well-being is intricately linked to our physical health, and understanding this connection is pivotal in the journey towards recovery. Holistic approaches to healing PTSD focus on nurturing both the mind and the body, recognizing that they are not separate entities but integral parts of a unified whole. By practicing techniques like mindfulness meditation, individuals can access the mind-body connection to alleviate symptoms of PTSD. Through these practices, individuals learn to ground themselves in the present moment, ease emotional distress, and reduce the physical tension often associated with trauma. Guided meditations, like the one provided below, offer a structured way to explore this connection, offering a path to inner peace and healing.

Guided Meditation for Healing PTSD

Here is a step-by-step table for a guided meditation to aid in the treatment of PTSD:

1. Find a Quiet Space: Select a peaceful environment free of distractions.

2. Comfortable Seating: Sit in a comfortable chair or cushion on the floor.

3. Relaxation Breathing: Close your eyes and take a deep breath in, counting to four, then exhale slowly, counting to six. Repeat several times to center yourself.

4. Body Scan: Begin at the top of your head and slowly scan your body mentally, noticing areas of tension or discomfort.

5. Release Tension: As you identify tense areas, visualize breathing relaxation into them. Imagine the tension dissolving with each exhale.

6. Mindful Awareness: Shift your attention to your breath, focusing on the sensation of each inhalation and exhalation.

7. Grounding: Feel the connection between your body and the support beneath you, anchoring yourself in the present moment.

8. Guided Imagery: Imagine a peaceful and safe place in your mind—perhaps a serene beach or a tranquil forest. Visualize yourself there, engaging all your senses.

9. Affirmations: Repeat positive affirmations or mantras related to healing and well-being. For example, "I am safe, I am healing, I am strong."

10. Gratitude: Conclude by reflecting on three things you are grateful for, no matter how small.

11. Slowly return to the present moment, gently opening your eyes when you are ready.

This guided meditation fosters a profound mind-body connection, offering a space for healing and self-compassion as you navigate the path towards recovery from PTSD.

Assignment: Begin a daily mindfulness meditation practice to reconnect with your body and mind.

Day 3: The Role of Nutrition in PTSD Healing

Nutrition plays a pivotal role in the healing journey for individuals dealing with Post-Traumatic Stress Disorder (PTSD). The food we consume not only nourishes our bodies but can significantly impact our mental and emotional well-being. A balanced and nutrient-rich diet can help regulate mood, reduce inflammation, and support overall resilience, essential factors in managing PTSD symptoms. Holistic nutrition for PTSD often emphasizes the consumption of foods rich in nutrients like omega-3 fatty acids, B vitamins, antioxidants, and complex carbohydrates. Additionally, it encourages mindful eating practices and lifestyle changes that promote a healthier relationship with food. Creating a food plan tailored to address PTSD is a powerful step toward holistic healing.

Creating a Food Plan for PTSD Healing

Here is an info table outlining how to create a food plan to address PTSD, along with nutrition habits and lifestyle changes:

Step	Instructions
1	Assess Current Diet: Begin by evaluating your current eating habits and food choices.

2	Consult a Nutritionist: Seek guidance from a registered dietitian or nutritionist who specializes in mental health and trauma-related issues.
3	Incorporate Nutrient-Dense Foods: Focus on foods rich in omega-3 fatty acids (fatty fish, flaxseeds), B vitamins (leafy greens, whole grains), antioxidants (fruits, vegetables), and complex carbohydrates (whole grains, sweet potatoes).
4	Mindful Eating: Practice mindful eating by savoring each bite, paying attention to hunger and fullness cues, and reducing emotional eating habits.
5	Hydration: Ensure adequate hydration by drinking plenty of water throughout the day.
6	Regular Meals: Aim for regular, balanced meals and snacks to stabilize blood sugar levels and mood.
7	Limit Processed Foods: Minimize the consumption of processed and sugary foods, as they can exacerbate mood swings and inflammation.
8	Herbal Teas: Consider incorporating calming herbal teas like chamomile and lavender into your daily routine to promote relaxation.

9	Lifestyle Changes: Support your nutrition plan with lifestyle changes such as regular physical activity, stress management techniques like mindfulness, and a consistent sleep schedule.
10	Track Progress: Keep a food journal to monitor how different foods affect your mood and overall well-being. Adjust your food plan accordingly.

By following these steps and embracing a holistic approach to nutrition, individuals with PTSD can take an active role in their healing journey, supporting their mental and emotional health through mindful eating and nourishing food choices.

PTSD Nutrition Guide with Ayurvedic and TCM Practices

Foods to Eat	Foods to Avoid	Ayurvedic Practices	TCM Practices
Omega-3 Rich Foods:	*Processed Foods:*	*Balancing Doshas:*	*Balancing Qi:*
Fatty fish (salmon, mackerel)	Fast food	Choose foods that balance your predominant dosha (Vata, Pitta, Kapha).	Focus on foods that nourish your specific Qi imbalances (Yin or Yang deficiency, stagnation, etc.).

Flaxseeds, chia seeds	Sugary snacks and drinks	Include warming or cooling foods, depending on your constitution.	Emphasize foods that move stagnant energy, such as ginger and garlic.
Walnuts	Highly processed foods	Opt for fresh, whole foods over processed options.	Incorporate Qi-tonifying herbs like astragalus and ginseng.
B Vitamins:	*Excessive Caffeine:*	*Digestive Fire:*	*Spleen Support:*
Leafy greens	Coffee	Enhance Agni (digestive fire) with spices like ginger and cumin.	Consume foods that nourish the Spleen Qi, such as root vegetables and grains.
Legumes	Energy drinks	Eat mindfully, savoring each bite. Avoid overeating or undereating.	Avoid foods that may weaken the Spleen, like cold, raw foods and dairy.
Fortified grains		Include fermented foods to support gut health and digestion.	Emphasize foods that tonify Qi, such as sweet potatoes and brown rice.

Antioxidant-Rich Foods:	Excess Sugar:	Stress Reduction:	Balancing Yin and Yang:
Berries	Sugary cereals	Practice stress-reducing techniques like meditation and deep breathing.	Incorporate foods that balance Yin and Yang, such as dark leafy greens (Yin) and warming spices (Yang).
Dark chocolate (in moderation)	Candy	Enjoy calming herbal teas like chamomile and lavender.	Balance your meals with a variety of colors, temperatures, and textures.
Green tea		Maintain a regular eating schedule to stabilize blood sugar levels.	Avoid extreme diets or excessive consumption of heating or cooling foods.

This table provides a holistic approach to nutrition for PTSD, integrating Ayurvedic and Traditional Chinese Medicine (TCM) principles. Remember that individual dietary needs may vary, and it's advisable to consult with a healthcare provider or practitioner of these traditions for personalized guidance. Balancing your diet with these practices can promote well-being and aid in managing PTSD symptoms.

Assignment: Create a balanced, PTSD-friendly meal plan for the week ahead.

Day 4: The Holistic Power of Movement in Healing PTSD

Movement is a powerful and holistic tool in the healing journey for individuals dealing with Post-Traumatic Stress Disorder (PTSD). Physical activity not only benefits the body but also has a profound impact on the mind and spirit. Engaging in mindful movement practices can help individuals reconnect with their bodies, release pent-up tension, and promote emotional well-being. Whether it's through yoga, Tai Chi, dance, or nature walks, holistic movement practices offer a safe and supportive space for processing trauma, reducing stress, and enhancing overall resilience. These practices foster a mind-body connection that can be transformative, helping individuals find a sense of grounding, inner peace, and empowerment. Below is an info chart outlining different examples of holistic movement to aid in the healing of PTSD.

Holistic Movement Practices for Healing PTSD

Movement Practice	Description
Yoga	Combines physical postures, breath control, and meditation to enhance flexibility, strength, and

	mental calmness. It offers a holistic approach to healing, integrating mind and body.
Tai Chi	A slow and gentle martial art that promotes balance, coordination, and relaxation. Tai Chi involves a series of flowing movements and is known for its stress-reduction benefits.
Dance Therapy	Utilizes creative movement to process emotions and promote self-expression. Dance therapy can be particularly beneficial for individuals who struggle to articulate their feelings verbally.
Forest Bathing	Also known as Shinrin-Yoku, this practice involves immersing oneself in nature. It can reduce stress, lower cortisol levels, and enhance overall well-being.
Qigong	A mind-body practice similar to Tai Chi, Qigong focuses on breath control, gentle movement, and meditation. It aims to cultivate and balance the body's vital energy (Qi or Chi).
Hiking and Walking	Simple yet effective, taking mindful walks in natural settings can improve mood, reduce anxiety, and provide a sense of tranquility.

Martial Arts	Disciplines like Karate or Judo offer physical conditioning, mental focus, and an outlet for pent-up emotions. They emphasize self-discipline and self-control.
Ecstatic Dance	A free-form dance practice that encourages uninhibited self-expression through movement and music. It can be a cathartic release of emotions.

These holistic movement practices serve as vehicles for healing and empowerment, offering diverse paths to recovery for individuals navigating the challenges of PTSD. The key is to explore and choose the practices that resonate most with your unique needs and preferences, creating a healing journey that is truly your own.

Assignment: Incorporate 30 minutes of physical activity into your day, whether it's yoga, Tai Chi, or a gentle walk.

Day 5: The Value of Good Sleep Hygiene for Healing PTSD

Good sleep hygiene is a cornerstone of healing for individuals coping with Post-Traumatic Stress Disorder (PTSD). Sleep plays a vital role in the body's ability to recover and rejuvenate, both physically and mentally. Unfortunately, PTSD often disrupts sleep patterns, leading to insomnia, nightmares, and restless nights. Addressing sleep disturbances is a critical component of PTSD treatment, as sleep impacts mood, cognitive function, and overall well-being. Establishing healthy sleep habits can significantly reduce symptoms and improve one's ability to manage the challenges of PTSD. Below is a chart featuring herbs, remedies, and recommendations to help improve sleep for individuals with PTSD

Improving Sleep with PTSD: Herbs, Remedies, and Recommendations

Herbs and Remedies	Recommendations
Valerian Root	Create a relaxing bedtime routine, including activities like reading or gentle stretching.
Chamomile Tea	Limit caffeine and alcohol intake, especially in the evening.
Lavender Essential Oil	Maintain a consistent sleep schedule, even on weekends.

Passionflower Extract	Ensure your sleep environment is comfortable, dark, and quiet.
Melatonin Supplements	Avoid heavy meals close to bedtime and opt for a light snack if necessary.
CBD Oil	Practice relaxation techniques like deep breathing or progressive muscle relaxation.
Magnesium Supplements	Consider therapy approaches such as Cognitive-Behavioral Therapy for Insomnia (CBT-I).
Limiting Screen Time	Keep a sleep diary to track patterns and identify triggers.
Herbal Sleep Blends	Engage in regular physical activity, but avoid intense exercise close to bedtime.

These herbs, remedies, and recommendations can be valuable tools in your journey to improve sleep while managing PTSD. However, it's essential to consult with a healthcare provider before trying supplements or herbal remedies, as they may interact with medications or have contraindications. Incorporating good sleep hygiene practices and exploring these options mindfully can contribute significantly to your overall well-being and the process of healing from PTSD.

Assignment: Establish a calming bedtime routine to improve the quality of your sleep.

Day 6: Cultivating Resilience in the Face of PTSD

Journaling can be a powerful tool for individuals dealing with Post-Traumatic Stress Disorder (PTSD) to build resilience and regain a sense of control over their lives. This exercise encourages self-reflection and personal growth. Objective: To explore and strengthen your resilience by reflecting on your experiences, emotions, and coping strategies.

Instructions:

- Select a Quiet Space:
- Find a comfortable and quiet place where you can focus without distractionsSet the Mood:
- Light a candle, play soft music, or create an ambiance that makes you feel at ease.
- Date Your Journal Entry: Begin by dating your journal entry to keep track of your progress. Reflect on Your Trauma:
- Start by acknowledging the traumatic event that led to your PTSD.
- Write about what happened, the emotions you experienced, and how it has affected your life.

List Your Current Challenges: Identify the challenges you face because of your PTSD. These can be emotional, physical, or social challenges.

- Explore Coping Mechanisms: Reflect on the coping mechanisms you've used to navigate your challenges. What has helped you? What hasn't? Be honest with yourself.
- Identify Resilience Factors: Write about instances when you displayed resilience. This could be times when you surprised yourself with your strength or when you overcame a difficult situation.
- Set Resilience Goals: List three specific resilience goals. These could include building a support system, improving self-care, or enhancing your coping strategies.
- Create an Action Plan: For each goal, outline the steps you will take to work towards it. Be realistic and patient with yourself.
- Express Gratitude: Write down three things you are grateful for today, no matter how small. Gratitude can enhance resilience.
- Self-Compassion: Show self-compassion by writing a kind and encouraging message to yourself. Acknowledge your strength and courage in facing PTSD.
- Daily Practice: Commit to journaling regularly. Make it a daily or weekly practice to track your progress, setbacks, and insights.
- Revisit and Reflect: Periodically revisit your earlier journal entries to reflect on your journey, celebrate your successes, and adjust your goals if needed.

- Journaling can serve as a therapeutic and empowering practice for those dealing with PTSD. It provides a safe space to process emotions, chart your growth, and cultivate resilience.

Remember that healing takes time, and resilience is a skill that can be nurtured and strengthened through self-awareness and self-care.

Assignment: Journal the above prompts and if you desire after you can decorate it, highlight or even burn your entry to release the energy.

Day 7: Creative Expression

The Healing Power of Creativity in PTSD

Creativity offers a profound avenue for individuals dealing with Post-Traumatic Stress Disorder (PTSD) to embark on a journey of self-discovery and healing. Engaging in creative outlets such as art, writing, music, or dance can serve as a means of self-expression when words fail to convey the depth of one's emotions. These creative processes enable individuals to explore their trauma, emotions, and inner worlds in a safe and non-judgmental space. Through creativity, individuals can regain a sense of agency over their experiences, find solace in self-expression, and connect with their resilience. It is a deeply therapeutic and empowering way to navigate the path toward recovery.

Art Therapy Assignment

The Healing Canvas

Objective: To use art as a therapeutic tool to explore and process emotions related to your PTSD, fostering healing and self-expression.

Materials Needed:

1. Canvas or thick paper
2. Acrylic paints, watercolors, or pastels
3. Brushes, sponges, or your hands for painting

4. A quiet and comfortable workspace

5. Optional: Music that resonates with your emotions

Instructions:

- Prepare Your Space: Create a comfortable and inspiring environment for your art therapy session. Light a candle, play soothing music, or simply find a peaceful space.

- Emotional Check-In: Take a few moments to check in with your emotions. Reflect on how you're feeling at this moment and any emotions related to your PTSD that you'd like to explore.

- Choose Your Medium: Select the art medium that resonates with you today. It could be acrylic paints for vibrant expression, watercolors for fluidity, or pastels for a softer touch.

- Start Freely: Begin to paint, draw, or create without a specific plan. Let your emotions guide your strokes and color choices. Don't worry about making it "look right."

- Express Your Emotions: As you work, think about the emotions or experiences you want to express. What colors, shapes, or symbols represent these feelings?

- Use Symbols and Metaphors: Incorporate symbols or metaphors that relate to your healing journey. These can be as abstract or concrete as you like.

- Let It Flow: Allow your creativity to flow without judgment or self-criticism. If you feel stuck, close your eyes, take a deep breath, and let your intuition guide you.

- Reflect: Once your artwork feels complete, take a step back, and reflect on what you've created. What do you see? What emotions have you expressed?

- Write About It: If you wish, write a few words or a short reflection about your artwork and what it represents for your healing journey.
- Self-Care: Take time for self-care after your art therapy session. Practice deep breathing, enjoy a warm beverage, or engage in any comforting activity that supports your well-being.

Remember that there are no right or wrong ways to create in this process; it's about the journey of self-expression and healing. You can repeat this art therapy assignment whenever you feel the need to explore and process your emotions related to PTSD creatively.

Assignment: Reflect on your process and creation below, look for 2-3 meaningful parts to you and journal in the space provided or in your own journal.

Day 8: The Healing Power of Sharing Trauma

Sharing one's trauma can be a deeply transformative and healing process. It offers individuals the opportunity to break free from the isolation that often accompanies trauma. When we share our experiences with a trusted and empathetic listener, we begin to release the heavy burden we've carried alone. This act of vulnerability can lead to a profound sense of relief, validation, and connection. As we externalize our trauma through storytelling, we gain a new perspective on our experiences and emotions, allowing us to process and make meaning of them. Through this sharing, we not only honor our own resilience but also pave the way for others to heal and find strength in their own narratives.

Narrative Therapy Assignment

The Healing Storyteller

Objective: To explore and begin healing from trauma through narrative therapy, a process that emphasizes the power of storytelling.

Instructions:

1. Choose a Safe Space: Find a comfortable and private space where you can reflect and share your story without interruption or judgment.

2. Set the Scene: Create a calming atmosphere. You may want to light a candle, play soft music, or have a comforting item nearby.

3. Write or Speak Your Story: Decide whether you want to write your story in a journal or speak it aloud. Choose the method that feels most comfortable to you.

4. Begin at Your Own Pace: Start your narrative therapy by recounting the traumatic event. Remember, there is no rush; go at a pace that feels manageable for you.

5. Express Your Emotions: As you share your story, express your emotions, thoughts, and physical sensations that arose during the traumatic experience.

6. Externalize Your Story: Separate yourself from the trauma by referring to it in the third person, as if you are narrating a story about someone else. This shift in perspective can be empowering.

7. Highlight Strengths and Resilience: Include moments of resilience, strength, and courage in your narrative. Celebrate your ability to survive and endure.

8. Reflect and Reclaim: After sharing your story, take a moment to reflect on how this process made you feel. What insights or new perspectives have emerged?

9. Self-Compassion: Practice self-compassion by acknowledging your bravery in sharing your story. Offer yourself words of kindness and encouragement.

10. Healing Symbol: Consider creating a symbol or image that represents your journey toward healing. It can serve as a reminder of your resilience and growth.

11. Safe Closure: Close your narrative therapy session in a way that feels safe and comforting to you. This might involve self-soothing, deep breathing, or grounding exercises.

12. Repeat as Needed: You can repeat this narrative therapy exercise as often as you feel comfortable and find it helpful. Each session may bring new insights and healing.

Sharing your trauma through narrative therapy is a courageous step toward healing. Remember that this process is deeply personal, and you have control over how much and when you choose to share. If you find that your trauma significantly impacts your daily life and well-being, consider seeking support from a therapist or counselor who specializes in trauma.

Assignment: Feel free to complete the above assignment in the space provided, online, on your phone, out loud, in your own journal or whatever feels right for you.

Day 9: Holistic Therapies for Treating PTSD

Holistic therapies offer a comprehensive approach to treating Post-Traumatic Stress Disorder (PTSD) by addressing the mind, body, and spirit. Studies have shown that holistic interventions can be effective in reducing PTSD symptoms and improving overall well-being. For example, mindfulness-based practices, such as mindfulness meditation and yoga, have been found to reduce anxiety and depression commonly associated with PTSD. Additionally, art therapy, acupuncture, and nature-based therapies like ecotherapy have shown promise in helping individuals process trauma and regain a sense of control. These holistic approaches empower individuals to connect with their inner resilience and promote healing on multiple levels.

Holistic Therapies for Treating PTSD

Holistic Therapy	Description
Mindfulness Meditation	Cultivates present-moment awareness and emotional regulation. Research indicates it can reduce PTSD symptoms, including hypervigilance and intrusive thoughts.

Yoga	Combines physical postures, breath control, and meditation to enhance overall well-being. It can alleviate anxiety, depression, and sleep disturbances in individuals with PTSD.
Art Therapy	Utilizes creative expression to process trauma and emotions. It provides a non-verbal means of communication and healing.
Acupuncture	Involves the insertion of thin needles at specific points on the body to balance energy flow. It can reduce anxiety and improve overall mood.
Ecotherapy	Engages individuals in outdoor and nature-based activities to reduce stress and promote emotional healing. It enhances overall well-being.
Aromatherapy	Uses essential oils to induce relaxation and reduce anxiety. Lavender and chamomile oils are commonly used to alleviate PTSD-related symptoms.

Research on Psychedelics and MDMA for Treating PTSD

Emerging research has shown promising results in the use of psychedelics, such as psilocybin (found in magic mushrooms), and MDMA (commonly known as ecstasy), in treating PTSD. Studies have indicated that these substances can facilitate breakthroughs in therapy by helping individuals revisit traumatic memories with reduced fear and emotional intensity. For instance, MDMA-assisted psychotherapy has demonstrated significant symptom reductions in PTSD patients, and psilocybin-assisted therapy has shown promise in reducing depressive symptoms in those with PTSD. However, it's crucial to note that these treatments are still in the experimental stage and should only be administered under the guidance of trained professionals in a controlled clinical setting.

Research on holistic therapies and the exploration of psychedelics offer hope in expanding the treatment options for individuals with PTSD. These approaches aim to provide relief from symptoms and promote lasting healing, ultimately improving the quality of life for those affected by this complex condition.

Assignment: Research holistic therapies such as acupuncture, aromatherapy, or massage, and consider incorporating one into your self-care routine.

Day 10: Emotional Release

Breathwork can be an effective tool for managing and alleviating symptoms of depression for several reasons:

1. Stress Reduction: Depression often coexists with high levels of stress and anxiety. Breathwork techniques, such as deep breathing exercises, activate the body's relaxation response. This, in turn, reduces the production of stress hormones like cortisol and triggers the release of calming neurotransmitters, promoting an overall sense of relaxation and emotional well-being.

2. Emotional Regulation: Depression is characterized by mood fluctuations and a sense of emotional overwhelm. Breathwork encourages mindfulness and self-awareness by focusing on the breath and the present moment. This can help individuals with depression recognize and regulate their emotions more effectively.

3. Reduction of Rumination: Depression often involves rumination, which is the repetitive and obsessive focus on negative thoughts and feelings. Breathwork can break this cycle by redirecting attention away from rumination and towards the breath, promoting mental clarity and reducing the intensity of depressive thoughts.

4. Improved Oxygenation: Shallow and rapid breathing is common in individuals with depression, which can lead to reduced oxygen intake and energy levels. Breathwork techniques emphasize deep and intentional breathing, improving oxygenation and boosting energy, which can be especially helpful in combating the fatigue associated with depression.

5. Enhanced Mind-Body Connection: Breathwork fosters a stronger connection between the mind and body. This can help individuals with depression become more attuned to the physical sensations associated with their emotions, allowing for greater self-understanding and emotional healing.

6. Coping Strategy: Breathwork provides a practical and easily accessible coping strategy that can be used anytime and anywhere. This empowers individuals with depression to manage their symptoms proactively and regain a sense of control over their mental health.

7. Stress Resilience: Regular breathwork practice can increase stress resilience over time. This means that individuals with depression may become better equipped to handle life's challenges and reduce the likelihood of depressive relapses.

Nervous System Response and Breathwork in PTSD

Post-Traumatic Stress Disorder (PTSD) often leads to dysregulation of the autonomic nervous system (ANS), which controls our body's involuntary responses. In PTSD, the sympathetic nervous system (SNS), responsible for the fight-or-flight response, can become overactive, leading to heightened anxiety, hypervigilance, and emotional reactivity. On the other hand, the parasympathetic nervous system (PNS), responsible for relaxation and restoration, can become underactive, resulting in difficulties with sleep, relaxation, and emotional regulation.

Breathwork techniques can play a crucial role in rebalancing the ANS in individuals with PTSD. Deep and intentional breathing can activate the PNS, promoting a state of relaxation and reducing the overactivity of the SNS. By focusing on breath, individuals can regain a sense of control over their physiological responses and create a calmer, safer internal environment.

Breathwork Techniques for PTSD

Breathwork Technique	Instructions
Diaphragmatic Breathing	Sit or lie down comfortably. Place one hand on your chest and the other on your abdomen. Breathe deeply into your abdomen, allowing it to rise and fall with each breath.
Box Breathing	Inhale for a count of four, hold for four, exhale for four, and hold for four. Repeat for several cycles, adjusting the count as needed.
4-7-8 Breathing	Inhale for a count of four, hold for seven, exhale for eight. Repeat this cycle four times.
Alternate Nostril Breathing	Sit comfortably with your spine straight. Close your right nostril with your right thumb and inhale deeply through your left nostril. Close your left nostril with your right ring finger and exhale through your right nostril. Continue alternating for several minutes.
Mindful Breathing	Focus your attention entirely on your breath. Observe each inhalation and exhalation without trying to change it. Simply notice the sensation of breathing.

Belly Breathing with Affirmations	Combine diaphragmatic breathing with positive affirmations. Inhale deeply, and as you exhale, silently repeat a positive affirmation like "I am safe" or "I am in control."

Assignment: Practice these breathwork techniques regularly, and pay attention to how they impact your nervous system response and overall well-being. Breathwork can be a valuable tool in managing the symptoms of PTSD and promoting a sense of calm and self-regulation.

Day 11: Native American practices for PTSD

Native American cultures have a rich history of holistic healing practices that can be valuable in addressing Post-Traumatic Stress Disorder (PTSD). While it's essential to recognize the diversity among Native American tribes and nations, some overarching traditional approaches and wisdom may contribute to the healing process. These can include:

1. Ceremonial Healing: Many Native American tribes have sacred ceremonies that connect individuals with their spiritual and ancestral roots. Participating in these rituals can provide a sense of purpose, belonging, and healing for those affected by trauma.

2. Talking Circles: Sharing one's experiences and feelings within a supportive community, often facilitated by an elder or healer, can be a powerful form of healing. Talking circles allow individuals to express themselves, receive empathy, and find validation for their experiences.

3. Sweat Lodges: Sweat lodges are used for physical and spiritual purification. The heat and steam create an environment where individuals can release emotional and physical toxins, promoting a sense of renewal and healing.

4. Herbal Medicine: Native American traditions often incorporate the use of herbs and plants for healing. Some herbs, like sage and sweetgrass, are used in smudging ceremonies to cleanse negative energies. Others may have properties that support mental and emotional well-being.

5. Counseling with Elders and Healers: Traditional healers and tribal elders can offer guidance, wisdom, and counseling to those dealing with trauma. Their cultural insights and spiritual perspectives can be invaluable.

6. Nature-Based Therapies: Many Native American cultures emphasize the connection between humans and the natural world. Spending time in nature, engaging in practices like wilderness therapy, or reconnecting with the land can be therapeutic.

7. Dreamwork: Dream interpretation and analysis are vital aspects of some Native American cultures. Exploring dreams with the help of a skilled dream interpreter can provide insights into unresolved trauma and facilitate healing.

It's essential to approach Native American healing practices with respect, cultural sensitivity, and humility. Seek guidance and permission from indigenous communities or healers when engaging in these practices. Additionally, consider integrating these approaches into a broader therapeutic plan under the supervision of mental health professionals experienced in trauma and PTSD treatment. Combining traditional wisdom with evidence-based therapeutic methods can provide a holistic approach to healing for individuals affected by PTSD.

Dreamwork Therapy Assignment for Healing PTSD

Dreamwork therapy can be a valuable tool for individuals seeking to heal from Post-Traumatic Stress Disorder (PTSD). Dreams often contain symbolic representations of our emotions, fears, and experiences, offering a window into the unconscious mind. This assignment encourages you to explore your dreams as a means of processing trauma and promoting healing.

Objective: To use dreamwork therapy as a tool for understanding and processing PTSD-related emotions and experiences.

Instructions:

- Create a Dream Journal: Start by setting up a dedicated dream journal. Keep it by your bedside with a pen or pencil.
- Intention Setting: Before sleep, set a clear intention to remember your dreams. Repeat a simple affirmation like, "I will remember my dreams tonight."
- Recording Dreams: As soon as you wake up, even if it's in the middle of the night, jot down any dream fragments, emotions, or images in your dream journal. Don't worry about making sense of them yet.
- Emotions and Symbols: Review your dream journal regularly and pay attention to recurring emotions, symbols, or themes that appear in your dreams. These may be related to your PTSD experiences.
- Symbolism Analysis: For each recurring symbol or theme, explore what it might represent in the context of your trauma. Consider the feelings it evokes and any connections to your past.
- Emotional Processing: Reflect on the emotions you experienced in your dreams. How do they relate to your waking life and PTSD symptoms? Journal about any insights or connections you make.
- Lucid Dreaming Techniques: If you have experience with lucid dreaming, consider using techniques to become aware and take control within your dreams. This can offer an opportunity to confront and change dream scenarios related to your trauma.

- Consult with a Therapist: Share your dream journal and insights with a mental health professional experienced in dreamwork and trauma. They can provide guidance, interpretations, and support.

- Artistic Expression: Consider creating art or writing inspired by your dreams. This can further help you process emotions and gain insights.

- Dream Re-entry: If a dream is particularly vivid or unsettling, try to re-enter the dream through visualization or meditation. This can allow you to explore it further in a safe environment.

- Respect Your Limits: If dreamwork triggers intense emotions or flashbacks related to your trauma, pause and seek support from a therapist. Your well-being is the top priority.

- Remember that dreamwork is a deeply personal and introspective process. It may take time to uncover meaningful insights and connections. Be patient with yourself and approach your dreams with an open heart and mind. Dreamwork can be a valuable complement to traditional therapeutic approaches in healing from PTSD.

Assignment: Explore the above assignment and write down any reflections you have or symbols that stand out to you. If you have, or were to imagine, a spiritual guide that might visit you in your dreams, who or what would they be?

Day 12: Creating Safety with PTSD

Finding and creating a sense of safety is a crucial aspect of healing from Post-Traumatic Stress Disorder (PTSD). Trauma often shatters our sense of security, leaving us feeling vulnerable and anxious. To begin the healing journey, it's essential to establish a foundation of safety—both in your external environment and within yourself. This may involve identifying safe spaces, people, and activities that bring comfort and calm. It also means developing self-compassion and self-soothing techniques to navigate triggers and distressing emotions. Safety is not just a physical concept; it's an emotional and psychological state that can be cultivated over time.

Assignment: Creating Your Safe Space

1. Select a Physical Space: Identify a physical space where you feel secure and at ease. This could be a room in your home, a cozy corner, or a natural setting like a park.

2. Personalize Your Space: Decorate this space with objects or elements that bring you comfort and joy. This could include soft blankets, soothing colors, calming scents, or cherished mementos.

3. Mindful Breathing: Spend some time in your safe space each day, engaging in mindful breathing exercises. Sit or lie down comfortably and focus on your breath. Inhale deeply, exhale slowly, and let go of tension with each breath.

4. Positive Affirmations: Incorporate positive affirmations into your daily routine. Stand or sit comfortably in your safe space and repeat affirmations like "I am safe," "I am resilient," or "I am in control." Believe in the power of these affirmations to reinforce your sense of safety.

5. Self-Compassion Journal: Dedicate a journal solely to self-compassion. Write down your feelings, fears, and achievements. Offer yourself words of kindness, understanding, and encouragement. Practice self-compassion as you navigate the ups and downs of your healing journey.

6. Create a Safety Plan: Develop a safety plan for moments when you feel overwhelmed or triggered. Identify specific coping strategies, emergency contacts, or calming activities you can turn to when needed.

7. Seek Professional Support: If you find that creating safety is challenging or overwhelming, consider working with a therapist or counselor who specializes in trauma and PTSD. They can provide guidance and support tailored to your unique needs.

Remember that creating safety is a gradual process, and it's okay to seek help along the way. Your well-being is a top priority, and cultivating a sense of safety within yourself and your surroundings is a significant step toward healing from PTSD.

Assignment: What makes you feel safe? What do you want to do to increase feeling and being safe? Can you identify one safe person in your life and why they are safe for you?

Day 13: Nature Therapy in the Treatment of PTSD

Nature therapy, also known as ecotherapy or green therapy, has emerged as a promising approach in the treatment of Post-Traumatic Stress Disorder (PTSD). This therapeutic modality recognizes the healing power of the natural world and the profound connection between human beings and their environment. Nature therapy involves guided outdoor activities, interactions with the natural world, and mindfulness practices in natural settings. For individuals with PTSD, engaging with nature can provide a sense of calm, safety, and connection—elements often disrupted by trauma. Nature's soothing and grounding qualities can help reduce symptoms of hyperarousal, anxiety, and intrusive thoughts. It offers a non-judgmental space for individuals to process their experiences, find solace, and regain a sense of control over their lives. By fostering a deep connection with the natural world, nature therapy complements traditional therapeutic approaches, contributing to the holistic healing of PTSD.

Here's a table with examples of nature therapy activities and their explanations:

Nature Therapy Activity	Explanation
Forest Bathing	Immersing oneself in a forest or wooded area, engaging all senses to connect with nature, reduce stress, and promote relaxation.

Nature Walks/Hikes	Exploring natural landscapes on foot, which can improve mood, increase physical activity, and offer a sense of adventure and discovery.
Gardening	Tending to plants and gardens, which provides a sense of purpose, connection to growth, and a soothing, mindful experience.
Outdoor Meditation	Practicing mindfulness, meditation, or yoga in natural settings, enhancing relaxation and self-awareness.
Wildlife Observation	Watching and connecting with wildlife in their natural habitats, fostering a sense of wonder and connection to the environment.
Nature Art and Creativity	Engaging in creative activities like drawing, painting, or photography inspired by natural surroundings, promoting self-expression and emotional release.
Campfires and Stargazing	Enjoying evenings in the outdoors by a campfire or under the stars, encouraging reflection, relaxation, and a sense of awe.
Canoeing/Kayaking	Exploring bodies of water in canoes or kayaks, providing a sense of tranquility, adventure, and connection with aquatic environments.

Nature therapy offers a diverse range of activities, each with its unique therapeutic benefits. Engaging in these activities can be a powerful adjunct to traditional therapies for PTSD, helping individuals find solace, reduce stress, and reconnect with the healing power of the natural world.

Assignment: Spend time outdoors, connect with nature, and engage in grounding exercises.

Day 14: Forgiveness and Self-Compassion

Assessing Progress on the Victim-Survivor-Thriver Spectrum

The purpose of this assignment is to help individuals with PTSD assess where they currently stand on the Victim-Survivor-Thriver spectrum. It can provide insight into their progress and guide their healing journey.

Instructions:

1. Self-Reflection: Set aside dedicated time for self-reflection. Find a quiet and comfortable space where you can focus.

2. Journaling: Use a journal or the space below to respond to the following prompts:

3. Victim Stage: Reflect on aspects of your life or thoughts where you might still feel like a victim. Write down any feelings of powerlessness, unresolved trauma, or negative self-perceptions.

4. Survivor Stage: Identify areas in which you have demonstrated resilience and a sense of control over your life. Write down the strategies, therapies, or support systems that have helped you become a survivor.

5. Thriver Stage: Consider moments or aspects of your life where you have moved beyond survival and are thriving. This might include personal growth, positive changes, or contributions to your community.

6. Scoring: Assign a score to each stage based on your reflections:

- Victim: 0-10 points

- Survivor: 11-20 points

- Thriver: 21-30 points

Interpretation: Reflect on your scores and where you fall on the spectrum. Acknowledge your progress and areas where you may want to focus on further healing and growth.

7. Seek Support: If you find that you are primarily in the victim stage or struggling to progress, consider seeking support from a therapist or counselor who specializes in trauma and PTSD.

Remember that healing from trauma is a journey, and progress may not always be linear. The goal of this assignment is to promote self-awareness and guide individuals toward a path of greater resilience and thriving as they continue their healing process.

Assignment: Goal Setting: Based on your assessment, set one or two achievable goals for yourself. These goals should align with moving further along the spectrum from victim to survivor and, ultimately, thriver.

Day 15: The Connection between PTSD and Our Bodies

Post-Traumatic Stress Disorder (PTSD) has a profound impact on our bodies as well as our minds. Trauma triggers a heightened state of physiological arousal, often referred to as the "fight-or-flight" response. When individuals with PTSD encounter triggers or reminders of their trauma, their bodies may react as if they are still in imminent danger. This can manifest as increased heart rate, shallow breathing, muscle tension, and a heightened state of alertness.

Over time, this chronic state of hyperarousal can take a toll on physical health and well-being, leading to issues like insomnia, chronic pain, and a weakened immune system. It's essential to recognize the strong connection between our minds and bodies when dealing with trauma.

Somatic Healing Assignment

Grounding and Self-Regulation

This assignment aims to help survivors of trauma, including those with PTSD, establish a sense of safety and self-regulation through somatic (body-focused) practices.

1. Safe Space Preparation: Find a quiet, safe space where you won't be disturbed. Ensure you're wearing comfortable clothing.

2. Breath Awareness: Begin by sitting or lying down in a comfortable position. Close your eyes if that feels safe for you. Focus your attention on your breath. Notice the natural rhythm of your inhales and exhales. Don't try to change your breath; simply observe it.

3. Body Scan: Start at the top of your head and slowly move your attention down through your body. As you focus on each area, notice any physical sensations without judgment. Pay attention to areas of tension, discomfort, or relaxation.

4. Grounding Technique 1 - Rooting: Visualize yourself as a tree with strong roots growing deep into the earth. Imagine these roots anchoring you and providing stability. Feel a sense of safety and connection to the earth.

5. Grounding Technique 2 - 5-4-3-2-1: Engage your senses to ground yourself in the present moment. Identify:

6. Five things you can see

7. Four things you can touch

8. Three things you can hear

9. Two things you can smell

10. One thing you can taste (or recall a recent taste)

11. Self-Soothing: Place one hand on your heart and the other on your abdomen. Take slow, deep breaths. Imagine sending warmth and comfort to yourself. Speak kind and reassuring words to yourself silently or aloud.

12. Regular Practice: Make this somatic practice a regular part of your self-care routine, especially during moments of heightened stress or when triggered by PTSD symptoms.

13. Seek Professional Guidance: If you find that somatic healing brings up overwhelming emotions or you struggle to self-regulate, consider seeking guidance from a therapist or counselor experienced in trauma and somatic therapy.

This assignment promotes somatic healing, which can help individuals with PTSD reconnect with their bodies, release tension, and regain a sense of safety and control over their physical responses to trauma triggers.

Journaling Assignment: After your somatic practice, journal about your experience. Note any physical sensations, emotions, or insights that arose during the practice.

Day 16: Herbal Remedies and Naturopathic Care for PTSD

A Historical Perspective

The use of herbal remedies and naturopathic care for addressing the symptoms of Post-Traumatic Stress Disorder (PTSD) has deep historical roots across cultures worldwide. Indigenous communities have long relied on the healing properties of plants to support mental and emotional well-being. Ancient systems of medicine, such as Traditional Chinese Medicine (TCM) and Ayurveda, incorporate herbal treatments and holistic approaches to address the impact of trauma on the mind and body.

In recent years, there has been a resurgence of interest in naturopathic and herbal approaches to mental health, including the management of PTSD. Research into the efficacy of herbal remedies like lavender, chamomile, and adaptogenic herbs has shown promising results in reducing anxiety, improving sleep quality, and enhancing overall emotional resilience. However, it's essential to emphasize that while herbal and naturopathic care can play a supportive role in PTSD management, they should be integrated into a comprehensive treatment plan that may include psychotherapy, medication, and lifestyle modifications.

Facts and Statistics

- Prevalence: According to the National Center for PTSD, approximately 7-8% of the U.S. population will experience PTSD at some point in their lives. This figure increases among certain populations, such as veterans and survivors of sexual assault.

- Complementary Therapies: Many individuals with PTSD seek complementary and alternative therapies, including herbal remedies, to alleviate symptoms. A study published in the Journal of Traumatic Stress found that over 40% of individuals with PTSD had used complementary therapies.

- Herbal Efficacy: Research suggests that certain herbs like St. John's Wort, lavender, and valerian root may have a positive impact on mood and anxiety levels. However, further clinical trials and research are needed to establish their efficacy conclusively.

- Holistic Approaches: Naturopathic care for PTSD often involves a holistic approach, addressing not only the symptoms but also the underlying causes of trauma. This may include dietary changes, lifestyle modifications, stress reduction techniques, and personalized herbal formulations.

While herbal remedies and naturopathic care offer potential benefits for managing PTSD, it's crucial for individuals to consult with qualified healthcare professionals who specialize in these approaches. The integration of naturopathic care should be done under the guidance of a healthcare provider as part of a comprehensive treatment plan for PTSD.

Below is a chart outlining some herbal remedies and instructions for their use:

Herbal Remedy	Description and Benefits	Instructions for Use
Lavender (Lavandula angustifolia)	Calming, reduces anxiety and promotes relaxation	Herbal Tea: Steep 1-2 teaspoons of dried lavender flowers in hot water for 5-10 minutes. Drink 1-2 cups daily. Essential Oil: Add a few drops to a diffuser or dilute with a carrier oil and apply to pulse points. Inhale the aroma.
Chamomile (Matricaria chamomilla)	Soothing, relieves stress and supports sleep	Herbal Tea: Steep 1-2 teaspoons of dried chamomile flowers in hot water for 5-10 minutes. Drink 1-2 cups daily, especially before bedtime.
St. John's Wort (Hypericum perforatum)	Mood stabilization, reduces depressive symptoms	Capsules: Follow the recommended dosage on the product label. Consult a healthcare provider before use, especially if taking medications.
Valerian Root (Valeriana officinalis)	Sedative, promotes relaxation and improves sleep quality	Tincture: Take 10-20 drops in water 30 minutes before bedtime. Start with a lower dose and adjust as needed. Capsules: Follow the recommended dosage on the product label.

Rhodiola (Rhodiola rosea)	Adaptogenic, reduces stress and supports emotional resilience	Capsules: Follow the recommended dosage on the product label. Rhodiola may take several weeks to show its effects. Consult with a healthcare provider.
Passionflower (Passiflora incarnata)	Calming, reduces anxiety and improves sleep	Herbal Tea: Steep 1-2 teaspoons of dried passion flower in hot water for 5-10 minutes. Drink 1-2 cups daily, especially before bedtime.
Lemon Balm (Melissa officinalis)	Calms the nervous system, reduces stress and anxiety	Herbal Tea: Steep 1-2 teaspoons of dried lemon balm leaves in hot water for 5-10 minutes. Drink as needed for relaxation.
Ashwagandha (Withania somnifera)	Adaptogenic, reduces stress and supports overall well-being	Powder: Mix 1/2 to 1 teaspoon of ashwagandha powder with warm milk or water. Consume daily or as recommended by an herbalist.

Safety Tips:

- Consult with a qualified herbalist or healthcare provider before starting any herbal treatment, especially if you are pregnant, nursing, or taking medications.
- Follow recommended dosages and guidelines for each herb.
- Monitor for any adverse reactions, and discontinue use if you experience any unusual symptoms.

- Keep herbal remedies out of reach of children.
- Herbal remedies should complement a comprehensive treatment plan for PTSD, which may include therapy and lifestyle modifications.

This chart provides a starting point for exploring herbal remedies, but it's important to individualize your approach and seek guidance from a qualified herbalist or healthcare professional for the most effective and safe treatment.

Assignment: Reflect on the information above and if you have ever used any above right about your experience or discuss with doctor or provider potential benefit of use.

Day 17: Guided Visualization for Healing PTSD

Guided visualization is a powerful tool for healing Post-Traumatic Stress Disorder (PTSD) as it allows individuals to safely explore and reframe traumatic memories, reduce anxiety, and cultivate a sense of control and empowerment. This technique can create a positive shift in how survivors perceive and process their traumatic experiences.

Here's a step-by-step guide to a guided visualization for PTSD:

Step 1: Preparation

- Safe Space: Find a quiet, comfortable space where you won't be disturbed. Ensure you're sitting or lying down in a relaxed position.
- Comfort: Make sure you're physically comfortable. You can use a cushion or blanket for added comfort.
- Breathing: Begin with a few deep breaths to relax your body and calm your mind.

Step 2: Grounding and Relaxation

- Body Scan: Start at your feet and slowly move your attention up through your body. As you do this, imagine a warm, gentle light moving through each body part, relaxing and releasing tension.

- Progressive Muscle Relaxation: Tense and release each muscle group, starting with your toes and working your way up to your head. Release all tension as you breathe out.

Step 3: Creating a Safe Space

- Imagination: Close your eyes and use your imagination to create a safe, serene, and peaceful place. This can be a beach, a forest, a meadow, or any place where you feel safe and relaxed.
- Sensory Details: Engage your senses by imagining the sights, sounds, smells, and sensations in this safe space. The more vividly you can imagine, the more real and comforting it becomes.

Step 4: Visualization and Reframing

- Traumatic Memory: Gently bring to mind a traumatic memory or emotion related to your PTSD. Picture it as an object or a symbol.
- Transforming the Memory: Imagine this object or symbol changing. It could dissolve, transform into something less threatening, or be encased in a protective shield.
- Empowerment: Visualize yourself as a strong, capable person who can manage this memory or emotion. See yourself in your safe space, holding the transformed object or symbol.

Step 5: Release and Letting Go

- Releasing: As you hold the transformed object or symbol in your safe space, imagine it slowly drifting away or dissipating into the atmosphere.
- Breathing: Take a few deep breaths, inhaling a sense of peace and exhaling any remaining tension or negativity.

Step 6: Returning to the Present

- Awareness: Gently bring your awareness back to your physical surroundings. Feel the ground beneath you and notice the room you're in.
- Open Your Eyes: When you're ready, open your eyes and take a moment to orient yourself to the present.

Step 7: Reflection and Journaling

- Self-Compassion: Be kind and compassionate with yourself, acknowledging the courage it took to engage with the visualization.

Guided visualization can be an essential component of PTSD healing when practiced regularly. It provides survivors with a safe space to reframe traumatic memories, reduce anxiety, and cultivate resilience. It's essential to practice guided visualization consistently and consider working with a mental health professional experienced in trauma therapy for additional support and guidance.

Assignment: Reflect on your guided visualization experience. Write down any insights, emotions, or shifts in your perception that occurred during the practice.

Day 18: Aromatherapy Remedies for PTSD

Cultures That Have Used Aromatherapy for Treating PTSD

Aromatherapy, the use of aromatic plant extracts and essential oils for therapeutic purposes, has been practiced by various cultures throughout history to address psychological and emotional well-being, including the symptoms of Post-Traumatic Stress Disorder (PTSD). Here are some cultures and traditions that have embraced aromatherapy for healing:

Traditional Chinese Medicine (TCM): TCM has a long history of using herbal medicine and aromatic plant extracts to balance the body's energy and address emotional imbalances. Aromatherapy is often integrated into acupuncture and other TCM practices to promote overall well-being and alleviate symptoms like anxiety and stress.

Ayurveda: The ancient Indian system of Ayurvedic medicine incorporates the use of essential oils and aromatic herbs to balance doshas (energies) and improve mental and emotional health. Aromatherapy is considered a valuable tool for promoting emotional balance and relaxation.

Indigenous Cultures: Many indigenous cultures around the world have used aromatherapy practices involving the burning of sacred herbs, resins, and woods as part of rituals and healing ceremonies. These practices are believed to cleanse negative energies and promote mental and emotional healing.

Egyptian Tradition: Ancient Egyptians used essential oils and aromatic plant extracts for various purposes, including embalming, religious rituals, and medicinal treatments. Aromatic substances like myrrh and frankincense were highly regarded for their therapeutic properties.

European Traditions: Throughout European history, aromatic herbs and essential oils were used for their healing properties. During the Renaissance, herbalists and alchemists developed various remedies that included aromatics to address emotional well-being and alleviate stress.

Aromatherapy Remedies for PTSD (Infographic)

Aromatherapy Option	Description and Benefits	Instructions
Lavender Essential Oil	Calming, reduces anxiety and stress, promotes relaxation	Diffusion: Add a few drops to an essential oil diffuser. Inhale the soothing aroma. Massage: Dilute with a carrier oil and apply to pulse points or as a body massage oil.
Frankincense Essential Oil	Grounding, reduces anxiety, and promotes emotional balance	Diffusion: Diffuse during meditation or relaxation. Topical Application: Dilute and apply to the wrists or temples.

Bergamot Essential Oil	Uplifting, relieves depressive symptoms, and reduces stress	Diffusion: Add a few drops to a diffuser to create a calming atmosphere. Inhalation: Inhale directly from the bottle or add a drop to a tissue and inhale.
Chamomile Essential Oil	Calming, reduces anxiety, and promotes restful sleep	Aromatherapy Bath: Add a few drops to a warm bath before bedtime. Diffusion: Diffuse during the evening to aid relaxation.
Ylang-Ylang Essential Oil	Mood-enhancing, reduces stress, and promotes emotional well-being	Massage: Dilute with a carrier oil and use in a relaxing massage. Diffusion: Diffuse to create a sensual and calming ambiance.
Cedarwood Essential Oil	Grounding, reduces tension, and promotes feelings of security	Diffusion: Use in a diffuser or inhale directly for a sense of stability. Topical Application: Dilute and apply to the skin as a calming oil.

Safety Tips:

- Always dilute essential oils with a carrier oil before applying them to the skin.
- Perform a patch test to check for any skin sensitivities or allergies.
- Use high-quality, pure essential oil from a reputable source.

- Consult with a qualified aromatherapist or healthcare professional, especially if you are pregnant, nursing, or taking medications.
- Store essential oils in a cool, dark place away from direct sunlight and out of reach of children.
- Discontinue use if you experience any adverse reactions.

Aromatherapy can be a valuable tool for managing PTSD symptoms, but it should complement a comprehensive treatment plan that may include therapy, medication, and other supportive practices. Individual responses to aromatherapy can vary, so it's essential to use these oils mindfully and consult with a healthcare provider if you have any concerns.

Assignment: Experiment with essential oils to create a calming environment in your living space.

Day 19: Affirmations and Their Role in PTSD Healing

Affirmations are positive statements that individuals repeat to themselves to challenge and replace negative or distressing thoughts. They can play a valuable role in managing Post-Traumatic Stress Disorder (PTSD) by addressing the cognitive and emotional aspects of trauma. Here's why affirmations can help with PTSD:

Thought Reframing: Trauma often leads to negative thought patterns and self-doubt. Affirmations challenge these thoughts and encourage more positive and constructive thinking.

Empowerment: Affirmations emphasize personal strengths, resilience, and the ability to overcome challenges. This empowerment can counter feelings of helplessness often associated with PTSD.

Stress Reduction: Repeating affirmations can induce a relaxation response, reducing the heightened state of arousal and anxiety common in PTSD.

Mind-Body Connection: Affirmations can improve the connection between mind and body, helping individuals become more attuned to their physical and emotional states.

Cultures That Have Used Affirmations

While the concept of using positive statements for mental and emotional well-being is universal, various cultures and traditions have incorporated affirmations into their healing practices:

- Hinduism: In Hinduism, mantras are chanted or recited as a form of affirmation to focus the mind, cultivate positive energy, and promote inner peace.
- Buddhists use affirmations as part of meditation practices to foster mindfulness, self-compassion, and a sense of interconnectedness with all living beings.
- Native American Traditions: Many indigenous cultures in North America use affirmations, often in the form of prayer or ritual chants, to promote healing, harmony, and connection with nature.
- Mindfulness and Meditation: Various mindfulness and meditation traditions from around the world incorporate affirmations as a means to center the mind and develop a positive outlook.
- Western Psychotherapy: In the field of psychology and psychotherapy, positive affirmations are widely used as cognitive-behavioral tools to challenge negative thought patterns and promote mental well-being.
- New Thought and Positive Thinking Movements: These modern spiritual movements emphasize the power of positive thinking and affirmations to manifest desired outcomes and improve overall life satisfaction.

Affirmations have a rich history and are integrated into diverse cultures and belief systems as a means of promoting mental and emotional well-being. Their effectiveness in managing PTSD symptoms lies in their ability to shift negative thought patterns and foster a more positive and empowering mindset.

Affirmations can be a powerful tool in your journey to healing from Post-Traumatic Stress Disorder (PTSD). This assignment is designed to help you create and practice personalized affirmations that can promote resilience, self-compassion, and a positive mindset. Here's how to get started:

Step 1: *Self-Reflection*

Take some time to reflect on your experiences and the specific challenges or negative thought patterns you face as a result of PTSD. Identify areas in your life where you would like to see positive change, whether it's related to self-esteem, anxiety, trust, or self-compassion.

Step 2: *Identify Positive Affirmations*

Based on your reflections, brainstorm a list of positive affirmations that directly address the areas you want to work on. These affirmations should be present tense, positive, and meaningful to you. For example:

"I am resilient, and I can overcome any challenge that comes my way."

"I deserve love, understanding, and healing."

"I trust myself and my instincts."

"I am safe, and I am in control of my life."

Step 3: *Daily Affirmation Practice*

Incorporate your affirmations into your daily routine. Here's how to do it:

- Morning Ritual: Begin your day by repeating your chosen affirmations in front of a mirror. Look into your own eyes as you say them with conviction. This can help set a positive tone for the day.
- Affirmation Cards: Write your affirmations on small cards and place them in visible places like your bathroom mirror, refrigerator, or workspace. Every time you see them, repeat them silently or out loud.

- Journaling: Incorporate affirmations into your journaling practice. Write them down, along with any thoughts or feelings that arise as you reflect on them.
- Mindfulness Meditation: During meditation sessions, focus on one or more affirmations. As you breathe in and out, repeat the affirmations in your mind. This can deepen their impact and promote relaxation.

Step 4: *Track Progress*

Keep a journal to track your progress. Note any changes in your thought patterns, emotions, or overall well-being. Celebrate small victories and be patient with yourself on days when affirmations feel challenging.

Step 5: *Adjust and Personalize*

As you progress in your healing journey, revisit your affirmations. Modify them to reflect your evolving goals and needs. Affirmations should grow with you and continue to support your well-being.

Assignment: Write down three affirmations to start with and see how they feel throughout this week.

Day 20: Trauma-Focused Yoga

Trauma-focused yoga is a specialized approach to yoga designed to support individuals who have experienced trauma, including those with Post-Traumatic Stress Disorder (PTSD). This therapeutic modality acknowledges the deep connection between trauma, the body, and the mind. It emphasizes safety, empowerment, and mindfulness in a trauma-sensitive environment. Trauma-focused yoga typically integrates traditional yoga practices with trauma-informed principles to promote healing and resilience.

Examples of Trauma-Focused Yoga Techniques and Explanations

Yoga Technique	Explanation
Gentle Poses	Trauma-focused yoga uses gentle, non-invasive poses to create a safe and comfortable experience for survivors. These poses help release tension and promote relaxation.
Grounding Techniques	Grounding techniques, like placing feet firmly on the ground, help survivors reconnect with their bodies and the present moment.

Breath Awareness	Focusing on breath awareness helps survivors regulate their physiological responses to stress and triggers. It promotes calm and self-regulation.
Mindfulness	Mindfulness practices encourage survivors to observe thoughts and sensations without judgment, fostering self-awareness and emotional regulation.
Somatic Awareness	Somatic practices guide individuals in exploring bodily sensations and emotions, facilitating the processing of stored trauma in the body.
Choice and Autonomy	Trauma-focused yoga prioritizes survivors' choices and autonomy. They are encouraged to modify poses or opt out of any activity that feels uncomfortable.
Supportive Environment	The yoga instructor creates a supportive, non-judgmental environment where survivors feel safe to explore their experiences and emotions.

This assignment encourages survivors of trauma, including those with PTSD, to engage in trauma-focused yoga techniques in a safe and supportive manner.

Instructions:

Safe Space Preparation: Find a quiet, safe space where you won't be disturbed. Use a yoga mat or a comfortable surface to practice on.

Gentle Warm-Up: Begin with a gentle warm-up. Start with slow, controlled breathing. Inhale deeply, exhale slowly, and focus on the rhythm of your breath.

Gentle Poses: Perform a series of gentle yoga poses. Examples include Child's Pose (Balasana), Cat-Cow Stretch (Marjaryasana-Bitilasana), and Legs Up the Wall Pose (Viparita Karani). Choose poses that feel comfortable and soothing to you.

Breath Awareness: Throughout your practice, maintain awareness of your breath. If you notice tension or discomfort, focus on your breath to ease these sensations.

Mindfulness and Somatic Awareness: During your practice, pay attention to bodily sensations, thoughts, and emotions without judgment. Allow yourself to experience whatever arises without trying to change it.

Choice and Autonomy: Remember that you have complete control over your practice. If any pose or technique doesn't feel right, feel free to modify or skip it. Listen to your body and prioritize your comfort.

Regular Practice: Make trauma-focused yoga a regular part of your self-care routine. Consistent practice can help you build resilience and reconnect with your body in a healing way.

Professional Guidance: Consider seeking guidance from a trauma-sensitive yoga instructor or therapist experienced in trauma-informed yoga if you find it challenging to practice alone or have specific trauma-related concerns.

This assignment encourages survivors to use trauma-focused yoga techniques as a tool for self-care, promoting healing and self-regulation in a safe and supportive environment.

Assignment: After your yoga practice, take a few moments to journal about your experience. Note any physical sensations, emotions, or insights that emerged during the practice.

Day 21: Energetic Healing for PTSD:

A Historical Overview

Energetic healing, also known as energy medicine or energy therapy, is a holistic approach to healing that focuses on the body's energy systems, aiming to restore balance and promote overall well-being. While it may not have a long history in the Western medical tradition, it draws upon principles and practices from various cultures and belief systems:

- Ancient Healing Traditions: Energetic healing has roots in ancient healing practices like Chinese Qigong, Indian Ayurveda, and traditional Indigenous healing methods. These traditions emphasize the flow of vital energy, or "qi," "prana," or "life force," within the body.

- Eastern Philosophies: Eastern philosophies, such as Traditional Chinese Medicine (TCM) and Ayurveda, have long recognized the importance of balancing the body's energy systems to maintain physical and mental health. Practices like acupuncture, acupressure, and Reiki are based on these principles.

- Modern Revival: The concept of energetic healing gained popularity in the West during the 20th century. Pioneers like Dr. Barbara Brennan (founder of Brennan Healing Science), Donna Eden (developer of Eden Energy Medicine), and Mikao Usui (founder of Reiki) played pivotal roles in bringing these practices to a broader audience.

Facts and Statistics

- Complementary Approach: Energetic healing is often used as a complementary approach to conventional medical treatments for PTSD. According to a survey published in the Journal of Traumatic Stress, individuals with PTSD may seek alternative therapies, including energy healing, to manage symptoms.
- Growing Interest: Interest in energetic healing for PTSD has grown, driven by anecdotal reports of symptom relief and a desire for holistic and non-pharmacological approaches to mental health. Research on the efficacy of energy therapies for PTSD is ongoing.
- Integration with Conventional Care: Many healthcare facilities are integrating energetic healing practices like Reiki and Healing Touch into their mental health and trauma treatment programs. This integration reflects the recognition of the mind-body connection in healing.
- Individualized Approach: Energetic healing approaches for PTSD are highly individualized. Practitioners often assess the patient's energy field and tailor treatments to address specific imbalances or blockages that may contribute to PTSD symptoms.

It's essential to note that while there is growing interest and anecdotal evidence supporting the use of energetic healing for PTSD, more research is needed to establish its effectiveness definitively. Energetic healing should be viewed as a complementary approach and integrated into a comprehensive treatment plan that includes evidence-based therapies, medication (if necessary), and the guidance of qualified healthcare professionals. Individual responses to energetic healing can vary, and its suitability may depend on personal beliefs and preferences.

Energetic Healing Therapy	Description	How It Works
Reiki	A Japanese technique that involves the laying on of hands to channel healing energy into the body.	Practitioners help balance the body's energy by placing their hands on or near specific energy centers (chakras) or areas of tension, promoting relaxation and healing.
Healing Touch	A biofield therapy that uses gentle touch or hand movements to influence the body's energy field.	Practitioners use their hands to clear, balance, and restore energy flow within the body, aiming to alleviate physical and emotional symptoms.
Qigong	An ancient Chinese practice that combines movement, breath control, and meditation to cultivate energy (qi).	Qigong exercises help improve the flow of qi through the body's energy channels, reducing stress and promoting overall well-being.

Pranic Healing	An energy-based healing system that uses prana (life force) to cleanse, energize, and balance the body's energy centers.	Practitioners scan the energy field and use specific techniques to remove stagnant or negative energy, allowing the body to heal itself.
Crystal Healing	Involves placing crystals or gemstones on or around the body to balance energy and promote healing.	Crystals are believed to have unique vibrational qualities that can influence and harmonize the body's energy, addressing specific issues or imbalances.
Sound Healing	Uses the vibrational qualities of sound, such as singing bowls, gongs, or tuning forks, to restore energy balance.	Sound waves resonate with the body's energy field, promoting relaxation, reducing stress, and facilitating healing on a deep level.
EFT (Emotional Freedom Techniques)	Involves tapping on specific acupuncture points while focusing on emotional issues to release blocked energy.	EFT combines elements of psychology and energy therapy to alleviate emotional distress and reduce the impact of traumatic memories.

Aromatherapy	Utilizes the energy and scent of essential oils to influence mood and promote relaxation.	Inhaling essential oils or applying them topically can have a calming effect, reducing stress and anxiety, which may help manage PTSD symptoms.

Note: Energetic healing therapies can be highly individualized, and their effectiveness may vary from person to person. It's essential to work with qualified practitioners who are experienced in the specific therapy of choice. Additionally, while these therapies may provide symptom relief, they should be considered as complementary approaches within a comprehensive PTSD treatment plan that may include psychotherapy, medication, and lifestyle modifications.

Assignment: Explore energy healing techniques like Reiki or Qi Gong to balance your energy.

Day 22: Laughter Therapy

Laughter Therapy for Healing PTSD

Laughter therapy, also known as laughter yoga or laughter meditation, is an approach to healing that utilizes laughter and humor as therapeutic tools. While it may not be the primary or sole treatment for PTSD, it can play a complementary role in managing symptoms and improving overall well-being. Here's why laughter therapy is considered healing for PTSD:

- Stress Reduction: Laughter triggers the release of endorphins, the body's natural feel-good chemicals. This can help reduce stress and anxiety, which are common symptoms of PTSD.

- Emotional Regulation: Laughter therapy encourages emotional expression and releases pent-up emotions. It can be a safe way for individuals with PTSD to process difficult feelings and experiences.

- Social Connection: Group laughter therapy sessions promote social interaction and a sense of community, which can combat feelings of isolation often experienced by individuals with PTSD.

- Mind-Body Connection: Laughter therapy combines physical and mental elements, promoting relaxation, improving mood, and enhancing the mind-body connection. This can help individuals with PTSD become more attuned to their bodies and emotions.

- Positive Coping Mechanism: Laughter can serve as a healthy coping mechanism to counterbalance the negative effects of trauma. It provides a break from intrusive thoughts and can improve overall mental resilience.

Facts and Statistics

- Endorphin Release: Research has shown that laughter can lead to the release of endorphins, which are natural painkillers and mood elevators. This physiological response can help reduce the intensity of PTSD symptoms.

- Impact on Stress Hormones: Studies indicate that laughter can reduce the levels of stress hormones, such as cortisol and adrenaline, which are often elevated in individuals with PTSD.

- Improved Quality of Life: Laughter therapy has been associated with improved quality of life, emotional well-being, and reduced depression and anxiety symptoms in various populations, including those dealing with trauma.

- Integration into Treatment: Laughter therapy is increasingly integrated into trauma-informed care and mental health treatment programs. It is used as a complementary approach to traditional therapies like cognitive-behavioral therapy (CBT) and exposure therapy.

- Group Dynamics: Group laughter therapy sessions can provide individuals with a sense of belonging and support, enhancing their overall mental health and resilience. This social aspect can be especially beneficial for those with PTSD.

Assignment: Watch a comedy show or spend time with people who make you laugh.

Day 23: Using Bilateral Stimulation for Self-Healing of PTSD

1. Select a Bilateral Stimulation Method:

- Walking: Walking stimulates our processing. Find somewhere comfortable with little distraction and think about the traumatic memory while walking. At the end of the walk consider how you would like to improve the way you think back on that memory.

- Tapping: Use your fingertips to gently tap alternately on your thighs, knees, or shoulders. As you tap, you can either focus on a specific traumatic memory or simply allow your mind to wander.

- Auditory (Binaural) Stimulation: Listen to binaural beats or bilateral sound recordings through headphones. These recordings produce slightly different frequencies in each ear, creating a sensation of movement and balance in the brain.

2. Set an Intention:

Before beginning, set a clear intention for the session. This might involve targeting a specific traumatic memory, reducing anxiety, or promoting relaxation. Having a purpose can help guide your experience.

3. Create a Safe Space:

Find a quiet and comfortable space where you won't be disturbed. Ensure you feel safe and relaxed before beginning the session.

4. Maintain Awareness:

As you engage in the bilateral stimulation, remain aware of your thoughts, feelings, and physical sensations. Notice any changes or shifts that occur during the process.

5. Allow Processing:

While engaging in bilateral stimulation, thoughts and emotions may arise. Allow them to surface without judgment. Focus on observing and processing rather than trying to suppress or control.

6. Self-Regulate:

If you become overwhelmed or distressed during the process, stop the bilateral stimulation and practice self-soothing techniques like deep breathing or grounding exercises until you feel more centered.

7. Journal Your Experience:

After the session, take some time to journal about your experience. Reflect on any insights, emotions, or changes you noticed during the bilateral stimulation. This can help you gain clarity and track your progress over time.

8. Consistency is Key:

Bilateral stimulation is most effective when practiced regularly. Set aside time for self-treatment sessions, but avoid overusing it to prevent emotional exhaustion.

9. Seek Professional Guidance:

While self-help techniques can be beneficial, they may not be suitable for everyone or all types of trauma. It's essential to consult with a mental health professional, such as an EMDR therapist, who can guide you through the process and ensure your safety.

Remember that self-help techniques are not a replacement for professional therapy when dealing with PTSD. If you find that your symptoms persist or worsen, or if you have difficulty managing your distress on your own, it's crucial to seek the support of a qualified mental health provider. They can provide personalized treatment and ensure your well-being throughout the healing process.

Assignment: You can journal about your experience of one of the above beliefs.

Day 24: Holistic Self-Care Routine

A self-care routine for Post-Traumatic Stress Disorder (PTSD) is an essential part of managing symptoms and promoting overall well-being. It involves a combination of physical, emotional, and psychological practices that help individuals cope with the challenges of living with PTSD.

Creating a self-care routine is an important aspect of maintaining mental and emotional well-being. Here are step-by-step instructions to help a therapy client develop their own self-care routine:

- **Set Clear Intentions:**

  Begin by understanding why you want to establish a self-care routine. Reflect on your therapy goals and identify what areas of your life you want to improve. These intentions will guide your self-care journey.

- **Assess Your Needs:**

  Take some time to identify your unique self-care needs. Consider the aspects of your life that require attention, such as managing stress, improving self-esteem, dealing with anxiety, or enhancing emotional resilience.

- **Consult with Your Therapist or Build On the Tools in This Book:**

  Prior to moving forward, it's advisable to have a conversation with your therapist about your desire to establish a self-care routine. Your therapist can offer valuable guidance and suggestions customized to your individual therapeutic objectives. If you do not have a therapist, utilize the tools and knowledge you've gained so far to craft your self-care routine while keeping the principles from the workbook in mind.

- **Identify Self-Care Activities:**

  Make a list of potential self-care activities. These can include relaxation techniques, hobbies, exercises, mindfulness practices, and social activities. Ensure that these activities align with your needs and preferences.

- **Prioritize Activities:**

  Prioritize the self-care activities that you believe will have the most positive impact on your well-being. Rank them according to importance and feasibility.

- **Set Realistic Goals:**

  Establish clear, achievable goals for your self-care routine. For example, if you're focusing on stress management, your goal could be to practice relaxation techniques for 15 minutes each day.

- **Create a Weekly Schedule:**

  Develop a weekly schedule or plan that outlines when and how you will engage in these self-care activities. Be realistic about the time you can allocate, and ensure you have a good balance.

- **Use a Journal or Planner or the Space Below:**

  Consider using a journal or planner to document your self-care routine. This can help you track your progress, set reminders, and reflect on your experiences and emotions.

- **Practice Mindfulness:**

Incorporate mindfulness into your self-care routine. Practice being present during your activities, and regularly check in with yourself to assess your emotional state and the effectiveness of your self-care practices.

- **Start Slowly:**

Begin with a manageable number of self-care activities, and gradually add more as you become comfortable and your routine becomes a habit.

- **Seek Accountability and Support:**

Share your self-care goals with a trusted friend, family member, or your therapist. They can offer support, encouragement, and accountability.

- **Adapt and Be Flexible:**

Be prepared to adapt your routine as you learn more about what works best for you. Some activities may need to be modified or replaced over time.

- **Review and Adjust Regularly:**

Periodically review your self-care routine with your therapist and make adjustments based on your progress and changing needs. Your self-care routine should evolve as you do.

- **Celebrate Achievements:**

Acknowledge and celebrate your successes, no matter how small they may seem. Recognize your commitment to self-improvement and self-care.

- **Practice Self-Compassion:**

Be kind and patient with yourself. Understand that self-care is an ongoing process, and it's okay to experience setbacks.

Your self-care routine is a personal and dynamic journey, and it's an essential complement to your therapy. Remember that self-care isn't selfish; it's a vital practice that supports your overall well-being and mental health.

Assignment: Create a personalized daily self-care routine that includes holistic practices.

Day 25: Connecting with Others

Connecting with others can be profoundly healing for individuals with Post-Traumatic Stress Disorder (PTSD) for several important reasons:

- Social Support: Connecting with friends, family members, or support groups can provide a crucial source of emotional support. Having a network of people who understand your experiences and are willing to listen without judgment can help reduce feelings of isolation and loneliness.

- Validation and Understanding: Talking with others who have experienced trauma or professionals who specialize in trauma can validate your feelings and experiences. It can reassure you that your reactions to trauma are normal responses to abnormal events.

- Reduced Stigma: Connecting with others who have experienced trauma can help reduce the stigma often associated with mental health conditions. It promotes open dialogue about PTSD and encourages individuals to seek help without shame.

- Shared Coping Strategies: Through connecting with others, you can learn valuable coping strategies from people who have faced similar challenges. These strategies can include relaxation techniques, mindfulness practices, and ways to manage triggers.

- Empathy and Compassion: Interactions with understanding individuals can provide a deep sense of empathy and compassion. Feeling heard and cared for by others can alleviate feelings of hopelessness and helplessness often associated with PTSD.

- Emotional Processing: Talking about traumatic experiences with trusted individuals can facilitate emotional processing. Expressing your feelings and thoughts in a safe environment can help reduce the emotional burden of unprocessed trauma.

- Social Engagement: Engaging in social activities or group therapy sessions can encourage individuals with PTSD to leave their comfort zones and participate in life more fully. This can counteract the avoidance behavior often seen in PTSD.

- Positive Distraction: Connecting with others can provide a welcome distraction from intrusive thoughts and memories associated with trauma. Engaging in enjoyable social activities can shift your focus away from distressing triggers.

- Sense of Belonging: Feeling connected to a community or group can create a sense of belonging and purpose. It can remind individuals that they are not defined by their trauma but by their connections and shared experiences.

- Safety and Trust: Building trusting relationships with others can help individuals with PTSD restore their sense of safety. Trust is a critical component of healing from trauma, and positive connections can contribute to rebuilding that trust.

Assignment: Join a support group or engage in online communities that focus on holistic healing for PTSD.

Day 26: Music Healing for PTSD

History and Cultural Context of Music Healing for PTSD

The use of music as a therapeutic tool for healing trauma and post-traumatic stress disorder (PTSD) has a rich history rooted in various cultures and traditions. Here is an overview of the historical and cultural context of music healing for PTSD:

- *Ancient Roots:*

  Music has been used for therapeutic purposes for thousands of years. Ancient civilizations, such as the Egyptians, Greeks, and indigenous cultures worldwide, recognized the power of music to evoke emotions, induce relaxation, and heal the mind and body.

- *Indigenous Practices:*

  Many indigenous cultures incorporated music and rhythmic rituals into their healing practices. Drumming, chanting, and singing were used to connect with the spirit world, release emotional pain, and promote well-being.

- *Traditional Eastern Medicine:*

  Traditional Chinese medicine and Ayurveda, an ancient Indian healing system, have long recognized the therapeutic qualities of music. Specific musical scales and rhythms were believed to balance the body's energy and promote harmony.

- *Western Music Therapy:*

  In the 20th century, music therapy emerged as a formal discipline in Western medicine. World War I and World War II highlighted the therapeutic benefits of music for veterans dealing with PTSD. Musicians played a crucial role in hospitals, helping wounded soldiers cope with physical and emotional trauma.

- *Sound Healing Practices:*

  Various sound healing practices incorporate instruments like Tibetan singing bowls, gongs, and crystal bowls to create resonant frequencies that promote relaxation and balance. These practices draw on ancient traditions and are used in modern holistic therapies.

- *Cultural Relevance:*

  Different cultures around the world have their unique musical traditions for healing. Native American tribes use drum circles and flute music, while African cultures employ drumming and chanting to connect with ancestral spirits. These cultural practices highlight the significance of music in healing and spirituality.

- *Contemporary Music Therapy:*

  Today, trained music therapists work with individuals with PTSD to address specific symptoms and promote emotional healing. Techniques such as lyric analysis, songwriting, and improvisation are used to help individuals process trauma and reduce symptoms like anxiety and depression.

- *Neuroscientific Understanding:*

  Modern research in neuroscience has shed light on how music affects the brain and can promote healing. Music has been shown to stimulate the release of neurochemicals like dopamine and oxytocin, which are associated with positive emotions and bonding.

- *Cultural Sensitivity:*

  When applying music therapy in a multicultural context, it's essential to respect cultural traditions and preferences. Music therapists often work collaboratively with individuals to select culturally relevant and personally meaningful music.

In summary, the history and cultural context of music healing for PTSD span across time and cultures. Music's universal and therapeutic qualities make it a valuable tool for promoting emotional healing, providing comfort, and fostering resilience in individuals dealing with trauma and PTSD.

Assignment: Listen, create, or experience music and reflect on the experience below.

Day 27: Cultivating Joy

Cultivating joy plays a vital role in healing from post-traumatic stress disorder (PTSD) by offering a pathway to emotional recovery and resilience. When individuals actively seek out and engage in joyful experiences, they counterbalance the overwhelming negative emotions associated with trauma. For example, finding joy in creative expressions like art, music, or writing can provide a means of processing emotions that may be difficult to express verbally. Connecting with loved ones, sharing laughter, and engaging in activities that bring happiness can rebuild social bonds and counteract the isolation that often accompanies PTSD. Additionally, experiencing joy can promote a positive outlook on life, increase emotional resilience, and provide moments of respite from intrusive thoughts and distressing symptoms. By incorporating joy into their lives, individuals with PTSD can gradually reclaim their sense of well-being and hope on their healing journey.

Assignment: Make a list of activities that bring you joy and plan to do one each day.

Day 28: Body Scan Meditation

What is a Body Scan?

Body scans, a mindfulness technique involving focused attention on bodily sensations, have shown promise in helping individuals with post-traumatic stress disorder (PTSD) through scientific research. PTSD often involves heightened states of arousal and hyperarousal, characterized by physical tension and the reliving of traumatic experiences. Body scans promote awareness of bodily sensations and can serve as a grounding technique to bring individuals back to the present moment. Research suggests that body scans can help reduce symptoms of hyperarousal, including muscle tension and increased heart rate, by promoting relaxation and calming the nervous system. Moreover, they encourage individuals to connect with their bodies, fostering a sense of safety and control that can be particularly beneficial for those with PTSD who may struggle with feelings of detachment or dissociation. While more research is needed, preliminary studies indicate that incorporating body scans into trauma-focused therapies can aid in symptom management and overall well-being for individuals grappling with the effects of trauma and PTSD.

Here is how to do a basic body scan:

Steps for a Body Scan	Instructions
1. Find a Comfortable Position:	Sit or lie down in a comfortable position. Close your eyes if you feel comfortable doing so.
2. Begin with Breath Awareness:	Take a few deep breaths to relax. Notice the sensation of your breath entering and leaving your body.
3. Start at the Top of Your Head:	Begin directing your attention to the top of your head. Focus on any sensations you notice, such as tension, warmth, or tingling.
4. Slowly Move Down Your Body:	Progressively shift your focus down through your body, part by part. Pay attention to sensations in each area, without judgment.
5. Notice Any Tension or Discomfort:	If you encounter tension or discomfort, simply observe it without trying to change it. Allow it to be as it is.
6. Breathe into Areas of Tension:	If you notice tension, take a deep breath and imagine the tension melting away as you exhale.

7. Continue to Your Toes (or Fingertips):	Work your way down to your toes (or fingertips), giving attention to each body part along the way.
8. Observe Thoughts and Emotions:	Throughout the body scan, be aware of any thoughts or emotions that arise. Acknowledge them without judgment and return to your body.
9. End with a Deep Breath:	After completing the scan, take a final deep breath and slowly open your eyes if they are closed.

Remember that consistency is key. Regular practice of body scans can help individuals build mindfulness skills that contribute to managing depression by fostering greater self-awareness, relaxation, and emotional regulation.

Assignment: Try a body scan meditation to release tension and promote relaxation. Write about your experience.

Day 29: Reflection and Gratitude

Reflection and gratitude play essential roles in the healing process for individuals living with post-traumatic stress disorder (PTSD). By encouraging introspection and self-awareness, reflection aids in emotional processing, helping individuals comprehend their responses to traumatic experiences. It also provides an opportunity to recognize personal strengths and coping mechanisms, fostering resilience. Gratitude, on the other hand, offers a shift in focus from negative aspects to positive elements of life, which can alleviate symptoms of depression and anxiety often associated with PTSD. Expressing gratitude not only enhances relationships but also reduces negative emotions, promoting emotional healing. While reflection and gratitude are not standalone treatments, they are valuable complementary strategies that, when incorporated into a holistic healing plan, can significantly contribute to the overall well-being and recovery of those dealing with PTSD.

Assignment: Reflect on your 30-day journey and express gratitude for your progress.

Day 30: Moving Forward

Setting and pursuing meaningful goals can be instrumental in the recovery process for individuals with post-traumatic stress disorder (PTSD). Research has shown that goal setting can provide structure and purpose, offering a sense of direction and control over one's life, which can be particularly empowering for those struggling with the unpredictability and chaos often associated with PTSD. Achieving goals, even small ones, can lead to a sense of accomplishment and self-efficacy, positively impacting self-esteem and confidence. Moreover, setting and attaining goals can help individuals rebuild their lives, reestablish a routine, and create a sense of normalcy, which are crucial steps toward healing and reclaiming a fulfilling life after trauma.

Here's a table outlining how to create SMART goals:

Component	Explanation
Specific	Clearly define the goal. What do you want to achieve? Be precise about what, where, when, and why you want to attain it.
Measurable	Establish concrete criteria to track progress and determine when the goal is achieved. Use quantifiable measures.

Achievable	Ensure the goal is realistic and attainable with available resources, skills, and effort. Avoid setting impossible goals.
Relevant	Ensure that the goal aligns with your values, priorities, and long-term objectives. It should be meaningful to you.
Time-bound	Set a specific deadline for achieving the goal. Having a timeframe creates urgency and motivation for timely action.

Using the SMART framework can help you create goals that are well-defined, manageable, and tailored to your unique circumstances, ultimately aiding in your journey to manage depression effectively.

Assignment: Set realistic, holistic goals for your ongoing journey towards healing.

Conclusion

Congratulations on completing the "Holistic Healing for PTSD" 30-day program. Remember that healing is a lifelong journey, and seeking professional help is crucial. By integrating these holistic practices into your life, you've taken a significant step towards managing PTSD and regaining peace and control over your life. Continue to prioritize your mental and emotional well-being, and know that you have the inner strength to heal and thrive.

About the Author

Krista (they/them) is a licensed therapist and the owner of Alternative Healing - Trauma and Psychedelic Integration Clinic. They hold a Masters in Social Work from Boston University and possess a wealth of experience in supporting survivors of trauma across various international settings, including the United States, Africa, and India. Their professional journey includes substantial engagement within community mental health, rape crisis centers, and other vital agencies, yielding profound insights into the intricate interplay between the body, spirit, and the mind's capacity for trauma recovery.

In pursuit of advancing their therapeutic expertise, they have undertaken a rigorous course of study, including their ongoing pursuit of a Ph.D. in Integrative Medicine. Their dedication extends to specialized training in areas such as Psychedelic Assisted Therapy, EMDR therapy, Somatic therapy, Trauma Focused Yoga, Nutrition, and an array of additional certifications aimed at furnishing individuals with an extensive toolkit to facilitate their personal healing journey.

Their unwavering commitment to their vocation is deeply rooted in their own journey as a survivor of childhood sexual abuse and other profound traumas that profoundly impacted their emotional well-being during their formative years. Their ardent mission revolves around empowering others to access the resources and strategies that can guide each unique individual in surmounting the obstacles hindering their path to healing.